Dulcitius
The Rising of the Moon
Every Afternoon
a trinity of short plays by women

DULCITIUS by Hrotsvitha
THE RISING OF THE MOON by Lady Gregory
EVERY AFTERNOON by Gertrude Stein

New Muses Theatre Company | Tacoma

DULCITIUS by Hrotsvitha, translated by Christopher St. John
THE RISING OF THE MOON by Lady Gregory
EVERY AFTERNOON by Gertrude Stein
Edited by Niclas Olson

Copyright © 2020 by Niclas Olson
All Rights Reserved

Printed in the United States of America
First Edition, 2020

ISBN-10: 1544155530

DULCITIUS, translated by Christopher St. John, first published in "The Plays of Roswitha" London, 1923

THE RISING OF THE MOON first published in "Seven Plays by Lady Gregory" New York and London, 1916

EVERY AFTERNOON first published in "Geography and Plays" Boston, 1922

This publication of DULCITIUS, THE RISING OF THE MOON and EVERY AFTERNOON may be used in its entirety, in adaptation or in any other way for theatrical production, amateur or professional, in the United States without fee, permission, or acknowledgement. (This may not apply outside the United States as copyright conditions may vary.)

All other rights, including electronic and digital reproduction, transmission and distribution, such as CD, DVD, the Internet, private file-sharing networks, information storage and retrieval systems, and photocopying are reserved.

www.NewMuses.com

CONTENTS

Dulcitius	1
The Rising of the Moon	25
Every Afternoon	49

Production History

DULCITIUS, THE RISING OF THE MOON, and EVERY AFTERNOON were presented on August 28, 2016 at the Dukesbay Theater in Tacoma, in a production by New Muses Theatre Company. The one night event was directed and designed by Niclas Olson. Sound was by Bethany Bevier. The cast was as follows:

DULCITIUS

DIOCLETIAN	Eric Cuestas-Thompson
AGAPE	Katelyn Hoffman
CHIONIA	Bethany Bevier
IRENA	Katherine Mahoney
DULCITIUS	Jeffrey Weaver
SISINNIUS	Niclas Olson

*other roles including soldiers, ushers, and the Wife of Dulcitius were played by members of the company.

THE RISING OF THE MOON

SERGEANT	Jeffrey Weaver
OFFICER	Eric Cuestas-Thompson
OFFICER	Katelyn Hoffman
MAN	Niclas Olson

EVERY AFTERNOON

Katherine Mahoney
Niclas Olson

Dulcitius
The Rising of the Moon
Every Afternoon
a trinity of short plays by women

DULCITIUS

by Hrotsvitha
translated by Christopher St. John

Characters

DIOCLETIAN — the Emperor
AGAPE
CHIONIA
IRENA
DULCITIUS — Governor of Thessalonika
WIFE — of Dulcitius
SISINNIUS
SOLDIERS
USHERS

Setting

Thessalonika. 304 A.D.

SCENE I

EMPEROR   The pure and famous race to which you belong and your own rare beauty make it fitting that you should be wedded to the highest in our court. Thus we decree, making the condition that you first promise to deny your Christ and sacrifice to the gods.

AGAPE   We beg you not to concern yourself about us, and it is useless to make preparations for our marriage. Nothing can make us deny that Name which all should confess, or let our purity be stained.

EMPEROR   What does this madness mean?

AGAPE   What sign of madness do you see in us?

EMPEROR   It is clear enough.

AGAPE   In what way are we mad?

EMPEROR   Is it not madness to give up practicing an ancient religion and run after this silly new Christian superstition?

AGAPE   You are bold to slander the majesty of Almighty God. It is dangerous.

EMPEROR   Dangerous? To whom?

AGAPE   To you, and to the state you rule.

EMPEROR   The girl raves. Take her away.

CHIONIA	My sister does not rave. She is right.
EMPEROR	This maenad: seems even more violent than the other! Remove her also from our presence, and we will question the third.
IRENA	You will find her as rebellious and as determined to resist.
EMPEROR	Irena, you are the youngest in years. Show yourself the oldest in dignity.
IRENA	Pray tell me how.
EMPEROR	Bow your head to the gods, and set an example to your sisters. It may rebuke and save them.
IRENA	Let those who wish to provoke the wrath of the Most High prostrate themselves before idols! I will not dishonour this head which has been anointed with heavenly oil by abasing it at the feet of images.
EMPEROR	The worship of the gods does not bring dishonour to those who practice it, but, on the contrary, the greatest honour.
IRENA	What could be more shameful baseness, what baser shame, than to venerate slaves as if they were lords?
EMPEROR	I do not ask you to worship slaves, but the gods of princes and the rulers of the earth.

IRENA A god who can be bought cheap in the marketplace, what is he but a slave?

EMPEROR Enough of this presumptuous chatter. The rack shall put an end to it!

IRENA That is what we desire. We ask nothing better than to suffer the most cruel tortures for the love of Christ.

EMPEROR Let these obstinate women who dare to defy our authority be laden with chains and thrown into a dungeon. Let them be examined by Governor Dulcitius.

SCENE II

DULCITIUS Soldiers, produce your prisoners.

SOLDIERS The ones you wanted to see are in there.

DULCITIUS Ye Gods, but these girls are beautiful! What grace, what charm!

SOLDIERS Perfect!

DULCITIUS I am enraptured!

SOLDIERS No wonder!

DULCITIUS I'm in love! Do you think they will fall in love with me?

SOLDIERS From what we know, you will have little success.

DULCITIUS Why?

SOLDIERS Their faith is too strong.

DULCITIUS A few sweet words will work wonders!

SOLDIERS They despise flattery.

DULCITIUS Then I shall woo in another fashion - with torture!

SOLDIERS They would not care.

DULCITIUS What's to be done, then?

SOLDIERS   That is for you to find out.

DULCITIUS Lock them in the inner room - the one leading out of the passage where the pots and pans are kept.

SOLDIERS   Why there?

DULCITIUS I can visit them oftener.

SOLDIERS   It shall be done.

SCENE III

DULCITIUS   What can the prisoners be doing at this hour of night?

SOLDIERS   They pass the time singing hymns.

DULCITIUS   Let us approach.

SOLDIERS   Now you can hear their silver-sweet voices in the distance.

DULCITIUS   Take your torches, and guard the doors. I will go in and enjoy myself in those lovely arms!

SOLDIERS   Enter. We will wait for you here.

SCENE IV

AGAPE   What noise is that outside the door?

IRENA   It is that wretch Dulcitius.

CHIONIA   Now may God protect us!

AGAPE   Amen.

CHIONIA   There is more noise! It sounds like the clashing of pots and pans and fire irons.

IRENA   I will go and look. Come quick and peep through the crack of the door!

AGAPE   What is it?

IRENA   Oh, look! He must be out of his senses! I believe he thinks that he is kissing us.

AGAPE   What is he doing?

IRENA   Now he presses the saucepans tenderly to his breast, now the kettles and frying pans! He is kissing them hard!

CHIONIA   How absurd!

IRENA   His face, his hands, his clothes! They are all as black as soot.

AGAPE   I am glad. His body should turn black - to match his soul, which is possessed of a devil.

IRENA   Look! He is going now. Let us watch the soldiers and see what they do when he goes out.

SCENE V

SOLDIERS   What's this? Either one possessed by the devil, or the devil himself. Let's be off!

DULCITIUS   Soldiers, soldiers! Why do you hurry away? Stay, wait! Light me to my house with your torches.

SOLDIERS   The voice is our master's voice, but the face is a devil's. Come, let's take to our heels! This devil means us no good.

DULCITIUS   I will hasten to the palace. I will tell the whole court how I have been insulted.

SCENE VI

DULCITIUS Ushers, admit me at once. I have important business with the Emperor.

USHERS Who is this fearsome, horrid monster? Coming here in these filthy rags! Come, let us beat him and throw him down the steps. Stop him from coming further.

DULCITIUS Ye gods, what has happened to me? Am I not dressed in my best? Am I not clean and fine in my person? And yet everyone who meets me expresses disgust at the sight of me and treats me as if I were some foul monster! I will go to my wife. She will tell me the truth. But here she comes. Her fools are wild, her hair unbound, and all her household follow her weeping.

SCENE VII

WIFE My lord, my lord, what evil has come on you? Have you lost your reason, Dulcitius? Have the Christ-worshippers put a spell on you?

DULCITIUS Now at last I know! Those artful women have made an ass of me!

WIFE What troubled me most, and made my heart ache, was that you should not know there was anything amiss with you.

DULCITIUS Those impudent wenches shall be stripped and exposed naked in public. They shall have a taste of the outrage to which I have been subjected!

SCENE VIII

SOLDIERS Here we are sweating like pigs and what's the use? Their clothes cling to their bodies like their own skin. What's more, our chief, who ordered us to strip them, sits there snoring, and there's no way of waking him. We will go to the Emperor and tell him all that has passed.

SCENE IX

EMPEROR I grieve to hear of the outrageous way in which the Governor Dulcitius has been insulted and hoaxed! But these girls shall not boast of having blasphemed our gods with impunity, or of having made a mock of those who worship them. I will entrust the execution of my vengeance to Count Sisinnius.

SCENE X

SISINNIUS   Soldiers, where are these impudent hussies who are to be put to the torture?

SOLDIERS   In there.

SISINNIUS   Keep Irena back, and bring the others here.

SOLDIERS   Why is one to be treated differently?

SISINNIUS   She is young, and besides she may be more easily influenced when not intimidated by her sisters.

SOLDIERS   That may be so.

SCENE XI

SOLDIERS We have brought the girls you asked for.

SISINNIUS Agape, and you, Chionia, take my advice.

AGAPE And if we do, what then?

SISINNIUS You will sacrifice to the gods.

AGAPE We offer a perpetual sacrifice of praise to the true God, the eternal Father, to His Son, coeternal, and to the Holy Ghost.

SISINNIUS I do not speak of that sacrifice. That is prohibited on pain of the most severe penalties.

AGAPE You have no power over us, and can never compel us to sacrifice to demons.

SISINNIUS Do not be obstinate. Sacrifice to the gods, or by order of the Emperor Diocletian I must put you to death.

CHIONIA Your Emperor has ordered you to put us to death, and you must obey, as we scorn his decree. If you were to spare us out of pity, you also would die.

SISINNIUS Come, soldiers! Seize these blasphemers and fling them alive into the flames.

SOLDIERS We will build a pyre at once. The fierceness of the fire will soon put an end to their insolence.

AGAPE O Lord, we know Thy power! It would not be anything strange or new if the fire forgot its nature and obeyed Thee. But we are weary of this world, and we implore Thee to break the bonds that chain our souls, and to let our bodies be consumed that we may rejoice with Thee in heaven.

SOLDIERS O wonderful, most wonderful! Their spirits have left their bodies, but there is no sign of any hurt. Neither their hair, nor their garments, much less their bodies, have been touched by the flames!

SISINNIUS Bring Irena here.

SOLDIERS There she is.

SCENE XII

SISINNIUS Irena, take warning from the fate of your sisters, and tremble, for if you follow their example you will perish.

IRENA I long to follow their example, and to die, that I may share their eternal joy.

SISINNIUS Yield, yield!

IRENA I will yield to no man who persuades me to sin.

SISINNIUS If you persist in your refusal, I shall not grant you a swift death. I shall eke it out, and every day I shall increase and renew your torments.

IRENA The greater my pain, the greater my glory!

SISINNIUS You are not afraid of being tortured, I know, but I can use another means that will be abhorrent to you.

IRENA By Christ's help I shall escape from all you can devise against me.

SISINNIUS I can send you to a house of ill fame, where your body will be abominably defiled.

IRENA Better far that my body should suffer outrage than my soul.

SISINNIUS When you are dishonoured and forced to live among harlots, you can no longer be numbered among the virgins.

IRENA	The wage of sin is death; the wage of suffering a crown. If the soul does not consent, there is no guilt.
SISINNIUS	In vain I try to spare her, and show pity to her youth!
SOLDIER	We could have told you as much. She is not to be frightened, and nothing can make her worship the gods.
SISINNIUS	I will show her no more mercy.
SOLDIER	That is the only way to deal with her.
SISINNIUS	Have no pity. Be rough with her, and drag her to the lowest brothel you can find.
IRENA	They will never take me there.
SISINNIUS	Indeed! What can prevent them?
IRENA	The power that rules the world.
SISINNIUS	We shall see.
IRENA	Yes! Sooner than you will like!
SISINNIUS	Soldiers, do not let the absurd prophecies of this woman interfere with your duty.
SOLDIERS	We are not likely to be frightened by a slip of a girl! We will carry out your orders at once.

SCENE XIII

SISINNIUS Who are these men hurrying towards us? They cannot be the soldiers who took away Irena. Yet they resemble them. Yes, these are the men! Why have you returned so suddenly? Why are you panting for breath?

SOLDIER We ran back to find you.

SISINNIUS Where is the girl?

SOLDIER On the crest of the mountain.

SISINNIUS What mountain?

SOLDIER The mountain yonder, nearest this place.

SISINNIUS O fools, madmen! Have you lost your senses?

SOLDIER What's the matter? Why do you look at us so threateningly, and speak with such anger?

SISINNIUS May the gods crush you with their thunder!

SOLDIER What have we done? How have we offended? We have only obeyed your orders.

SISINNIUS Fools! Did I not tell you to take this rebellious girl to a brothel?

SOLDIER That is so, but while we were on the way up came two young strangers and told us you had sent them to take Irena to the summit of the mountain.

SISINNIUS   I learn this for the first time from you.

SOLDIER   So we see.

SISINNIUS   What were these strangers like?

SOLDIER   They were gorgeously dressed and looked like people of rank.

SISINNIUS   Did you not follow them?

SOLDIER   Yes, we followed them.

SISINNIUS   What did they do?

SOLDIER   They placed themselves one on each side of Irena, and told us to hasten and tell you what we had seen.

SISINNIUS   Then there is nothing to do but for me to mount my horse and ride to the mountain to discover who has dared to play us this trick.

SOLDIERS   We will come too.

SCENE XIV

SISINNIUS   What has happened to me? These Christians have bewitched me. I wander blindly round this hill, and when I stumble on a path I can neither follow it nor return upon my steps.

SOLDIER   We are all the sport of some strange enchantment. We are exhausted. If you let this madwoman live an hour longer it will be the death of us all.

SISINNIUS   Take a bow one of you, bend it as far as you can, and loose a shaft that shall pierce this devilish witch.

SOLDIER   That's the way!

IRENA   You wretched Sisinnius! Do you not blush for your shameful defeat? Are you not ashamed that you could not overcome the resolution of a little child without resorting to force of arms?

SISINNIUS   I accept the shame gladly, since now I am sure of your death.

IRENA   To me my death means joy, but to you calamity. For your cruelty you will be damned in Tartarus. But I shall receive the martyr's palm, and adorned with the crown of virginity, I shall enter the azure palace of the Eternal King, to Whom be glory and honour for ever and ever!

THE RISING OF THE MOON

by Lady Gregory

Characters

SERGEANT
OFFICER B
OFFICER X
MAN   a ballad singer

Setting

Side of a quay in a seaport town. Ireland.

Moonlight. Some posts and chains. A large barrel. Enter three policemen.

Sergeant, who is older than the others, crosses the stage to right and looks down steps. The others put down a paste-pot and unroll a bundle of placards.

OFFICER B   I think this would be a good place to put up a notice. (*he points to barrel*)

OFFICER X   Better ask him. (*calls to Sergeant*) Will this be a good place for a placard?

No answer

OFFICER B   Will we put up a notice here on the barrel?

No answer

SERGEANT   There's a flight of steps here that leads to the water. This is a place that should be minded well. If he got down here, his friends might have a boat to meet him; they might send it in here from outside.

OFFICER B   Would the barrel be a good place to put a notice up?

SERGEANT   It might; you can put it there.

They paste the notice up

SERGEANT (*reading*) Dark hair - dark eyes, smooth face, height five feet five - there's not much to take hold of in that - It's a pity I had no chance of seeing him before he broke out of gaol. They say he's a wonder, that it's he makes all the plans for the whole organization. There isn't another man in Ireland would have broken gaol the way he did. He must have some friends among the gaolers.

OFFICER B A hundred pounds is little enough for the Government to offer for him. You may be sure any man in the force that takes him will get promotion.

SERGEANT I'll mind this place myself. I wouldn't wonder at all if he came this way. He might come slipping along there (*points to side of quay*), and his friends might be waiting for him there (*points down steps*), and once he got away it's little chance we'd have of finding him; it's maybe under a load of kelp he'd be in a fishing boat, and not one to help a married man that wants it to the reward.

OFFICER X And if we get him itself, nothing but abuse on our heads for it from the people, and maybe from our own relations.

SERGEANT Well, we have to do our duty in the force. Haven't we the whole country depending on us to keep law and order? It's those that are down would be up and those that are up would be down, if it wasn't for us. Well, hurry on, you have plenty of other places to placard yet, and come back here then to me. You can take the lantern. Don't be too long now. It's very lonesome here with nothing but the moon.

OFFICER B   It's a pity we can't stop with you. The Government should have brought more police into the town, with him in gaol, and at assizel time too. Well, good luck to your watch.

They go out.

SERGEANT (*walks up and down once or twice and looks at placard*) A hundred pounds and promotion sure. There must be a great deal of spending in a hundred pounds. It's a pity some honest man not to be better of that.

A ragged man appears at left and tries to slip past. Sergeant suddenly turns.

SERGEANT   Where are you going?

MAN   I'm a poor ballad-singer, your honor. I thought to sell some of these (*holds out bundle of ballads*) to the sailors. (*he goes on*)

SERGEANT Stop! Didn't I tell you to stop? You can't go on there.

MAN Oh, very well. It's a hard thing to be poor. All the world's against the poor!

SERGEANT Who are you?

MAN You'd be as wise as myself if I told you, but I don't mind. I'm one Jimmy Walsh, a ballad-singer.

SERGEANT Jimmy Walsh? I don't know that name.

MAN Ah, sure, they know it well enough in Ennis. Were you ever in Ennis, sergeant?

SERGEANT What brought you here?

MAN Sure, it's to the assizes I came, thinking I might make a few shillings here or there. It's in the one train with the judges I came.

SERGEANT Well, if you came so far, you may as well go farther, for you'll walk out of this.

MAN I will, I will; I'll just go on where I was going. (*goes toward steps*)

SERGEANT Come back from those steps; no one has leave to pass down them to-night.

MAN I'll just sit on the top of the steps till I see will some sailor buy a ballad off me that would give me my supper. They do be late going

                    back to the ship. It's often I saw them in Cork
                    carried down the quay in a handcart.

SERGEANT Move on, I tell you. I won't have anyone
                    lingering about the quay tonight.

MAN   Well, I'll go. It's the poor have the hard life!
                    Maybe yourself might like one, sergeant.
                    Here's a good sheet now. (*turns one over*)
                    "Content and a pipe" - that's not much. "The
                    Peeler and the goat" - you wouldn't like that.
                    "Johnny Hart" - that's a lovely song.

SERGEANT Move on.

MAN   Ah, wait till you hear it.
                    (*sings*)
                    There was a rich farmer's daughter lived near
                        the town of Ross;
                    She courted a Highland soldier, his name was
                        Johnny Hart;
                    Says the mother to her daughter, "I'll go
                        distracted mad
                    If you marry that Highland soldier dressed up
                        in Highland plaid."

SERGEANT Stop that noise.

Man wraps up his ballads and shuffles towards the steps.

SERGEANT Where are you going?

MAN   Sure you told me to be going, and I am
                    going.

SERGEANT Don't be a fool. I didn't tell you to go that way; I told you to go back to the town.

MAN Back to the town, is it?

SERGEANT (*taking him by the shoulder and shoving him before him*) Here, I'll show you the way. Be off with you. What are you stopping for?

MAN (*who has been keeping his eye on the notice, points to it*) I think I know what you're waiting for, sergeant.

SERGEANT What's that to you?

MAN And I know well the man you're waiting for - I know him well - I'll be going. (*he shuffles on*)

SERGEANT You know him? Come back here. What sort is he?

MAN Come back is it, sergeant? Do you want to have me killed?

SERGEANT Why do you say that?

MAN Never mind. I'm going. I wouldn't be in your shoes if the reward was ten times as much. (*goes on offstage to left*) Not if it was ten times as much.

SERGEANT (*rushing after him*) Come back here, come back. (*drags him back*) What sort is he? Where did you see him?

MAN I saw him in my own place, in the County Clare. I tell you you wouldn't like to be looking at him. You'd be afraid to be in the one place with him. There isn't a weapon he doesn't know the use of, and as to strength, his muscles are as hard as that board. (*slaps barrel*)

SERGEANT Is he as bad as that?

MAN He is then.

SERGEANT Do you tell me so?

MAN There was a poor man in our place, a sergeant from Ballyvaughan. - It was with a lump of stone he did it.

SERGEANT I never heard of that.

MAN And you wouldn't, sergeant. It's not everything that happens gets into the papers. And there was a policeman in plain clothes, too... It is in Limerick he was... It was after the time of the attack on the police barrack in Kilmallock... Moonlight... just like this..., waterside... Nothing was known for certain.

SERGEANT Do you say so? It's a terrible country to belong to.

MAN That's so, indeed! You might be standing there, looking out that way, thinking you saw him coming up this side of the quay (*points*), and he might be coming up this other side (*points*), and he'd be on you before you knew where you were.

SERGEANT   It's a whole troop of police they ought to put here to stop a man like that.

MAN   But if you'd like me to stop with you, I could be looking down this side. I could be sitting up here on this barrel.

SERGEANT   And you know him well, too?

MAN   I'd know him a mile off, sergeant.

SERGEANT   But you wouldn't want to share the reward?

MAN   Is it a poor man like me, that has to be going the roads and singing in fairs, to have the name on him that he took a reward? But you don't want me. I'll be safer in the town.

SERGEANT   Well, you can stop.

MAN   (*getting up on barrel*) All right, sergeant, I wonder now, you're tired out, sergeant, walking up and down the way you are.

SERGEANT   If I'm tired I'm used to it.

MAN   You might have hard work before you tonight yet. Take it easy while you can. There's plenty of room up here on the barrel, and you see farther when you're higher up.

SERGEANT   Maybe so.

Gets up beside him on barrel, facing right. They sit back to back, looking different ways.

SERGEANT You made me feel a bit queer with the way you talked.

MAN Give me a match, sergeant; (*he gives it and Man lights pipe*) take a draw yourself? It'll quiet you. Wait now till I give you a light, but you needn't turn round. Don't take your eye off the quay for the life of you.

SERGEANT Never fear, I won't. (*lights pipe, they both smoke*) Indeed it's a hard thing to be in the force, out at night and no thanks for it, for all the danger we're in. And it's little we get but abuse from the people, and no choice but to obey our orders, and never asked when a man is sent into danger, if you are a married man with a family.

MAN (*sings*) As through the hills I walked to view the hills and shamrock plain,
I stood awhile where nature smiles to view the rocks and streams,
On a matron fair I fixed my eyes beneath a fertile vale,
And she sang her song it was on the wrong of poor old Granuaile.

SERGEANT Stop that; that's no song to be singing in these times.

MAN Ah, sergeant, I was only singing to keep my heart up. It sinks when I think of him. To think of us two sitting here, and he creeping up the quay, maybe, to get to us.

SERGEANT Are you keeping a good lookout?

MAN I am; and for no reward too. Amn't I the foolish man? But when I saw a man in trouble, I never could help trying to get him out of it. What's that? Did something hit me? (*rubs his heart*)

SERGEANT (*patting him on the shoulder*) You will get your reward in heaven.

MAN I know that, I know that, sergeant, but life is precious.

SERGEANT Well, you can sing if it gives you more courage.

MAN (*sings*) Her head was bare, her hands and feet with iron bands were bound,
Her pensive strain and plaintive wail mingles with the evening gale
And the song she sang with mournful air, I am old Granuaile.
Her lips so sweet that monarchs kissed...

SERGEANT That's not it... "Her gown she wore was stained with gore."... That's it - you missed that.

MAN You're right, sergeant, so it is, I missed it. (*repeats line*) But to think of a man like you knowing a song like that.

SERGEANT There's many a thing a man might know and might not have any wish for.

MAN Now, I daresay, sergeant, in your youth, you used to be sitting up on a wall, the way you are sitting up on this barrel now, and the other lads beside you, and you singing "Granuaile"?...

SERGEANT I did then.

MAN And the "Shan Van Vocht"?...

SERGEANT I did then.

MAN And the "Green on the Cape?"

SERGEANT That was one of them.

MAN And maybe the man you are watching for tonight used to be sitting on the wall, when he was young, and singing those same songs.... It's a queer world....

SERGEANT Whisht!... I think I see something coming.... It's only a dog.

MAN And isn't it a queer world?... Maybe it's one of the boys you used to be singing with that time you will be arresting today or tomorrow, and sending into the dock....

SERGEANT That's true indeed.

MAN And maybe one night, after you had been singing, if the other boys had told you some plan they had, some plan to free the country, you might have joined with them..., and maybe it is you might be in trouble now.

SERGEANT Well, who knows but I might? I had a great spirit in those days.

MAN It's a queer world, sergeant, and it's little any mother knows when she sees her child creeping on the floor what might happen to it before it has gone through its life, or who will be who in the end.

SERGEANT That's a queer thought now, and a true thought. Wait now till I think it out. If it wasn't for the sense I have, and for my wife and family, and for me joining the force the time I did, it might be myself now would be after breaking gaol and hiding in the dark, and it might be him that's hiding in the dark and that got out of gaol would be sitting up here where I am on this barrel.... And it might be myself would be creeping up trying to make my escape from himself, and it might be himself would be keeping the law, and myself would be breaking it, and myself would be trying to put a bullet in his head or to take up a lump of stone the way you said he did... no, that myself did... Oh! (*gasps, after a pause*) What's that? (*grasps Man's arm*)

MAN (*jumps off barrel and listens, looking out over water*) It's nothing, sergeant.

SERGEANT I thought it might be a boat. I had a notion there might be friends of his coming about the quays with a boat.

MAN Sergeant, I am thinking it was with the people you were, and not with the law you were, when you were a young man.

SERGEANT Well, if I was foolish then, that time's gone.

MAN Maybe, sergeant, it comes into your head sometimes, in spite of your belt and your tunic, that it might have been as well for you to have followed Granuaile.

SERGEANT It's no business of yours what I think.

MAN Maybe, sergeant, you'll be on the side of the country yet.

SERGEANT (*gets off barrel*). Don't talk to me like that. I have my duties and I know them. (*looks round*) That was a boat; I hear the oars. (*goes to the steps and looks down*)

MAN (*sings*) O, then, tell me, Shawn O'Farrell,
Where the gathering is to be.
In the old spot by the river
Right well known to you and me!

SERGEANT Stop that! Stop that, I tell you!

MAN (*sings louder*) One word more, for signal token,
Whistle up the marching tune,

> With your pike upon your shoulder,
> At the Rising of the Moon.

SERGEANT If you don t stop that, I'll arrest you.

A whistle from below answers, repeating the air.

SERGEANT That's a signal. (*stands between him and steps*) You must not pass this way.... Step farther back.... Who are you? You are no ballad-singer.

MAN You needn't ask who I am - that placard will tell you. (*points to placard*)

SERGEANT You are the man I am looking for.

MAN (*takes off hat and wig, Sergeant seizes them*) I am. There's a hundred pounds on my head. There is a friend of mine below in a boat. He knows a safe place to bring me to.

SERGEANT (*looking still at hat and wig*) It's a pity! It's a pity. You deceived me. You deceived me well.

MAN I am a friend of Granuaile. There is a hundred pounds on my head.

SERGEANT It's a pity, it's a pity!

MAN Will you let me pass, or must I make you let me?

SERGEANT   I am in the force. I will not let you pass.

MAN   I thought to do it with my tongue. (*puts hand in breast*) What is that?

OFFICER X   (*offstage*) Here, this is where we left him.

SERGEANT   It's my comrades coming.

MAN   You won't betray me... the friend of Granuaile. (*slips behind barrel*)

OFFICER B   (*offstage*) That was the last of the placards.

OFFICER X   (*as they come in*) If he makes his escape it won't be unknown he'll make it.

Sergeant puts hat and wig behind his back.

OFFICER B   Did any one come this way?

SERGEANT   (*after a pause*) No one.

OFFICER B   No one at all?

SERGEANT   No one at all.

OFFICER B   We had no orders to go back to the station; we can stop along with you.

SERGEANT   I don't want you. There is nothing for you to do here.

OFFICER B   You bade us to come back here and keep watch with you.

SERGEANT I'd sooner be alone. Would any man come this way and you making all that talk? It is better the place to be quiet.

OFFICER B Well, we'll leave you the lantern anyhow. (*hands it to him*)

SERGEANT I don't want it. Bring it with you.

OFFICER B You might want it. There are clouds coming up and you have the darkness of the night before you yet. I'll leave it over here on the barrel. (*goes to barrel*)

SERGEANT Bring it with you I tell you. No more talk.

OFFICER B Well, I thought it might be a comfort to you. I often think when I have it in my hand and can be flashing it about into every dark corner (*doing so*) that it's the same as being beside the fire at home, and the bits of bogwood blazing up now and again. (*flashes it about, now on the barrel, now on Sergeant*)

SERGEANT (*furious*) Be off the two of you, yourselves and your lantern!

They go out. Man comes from behind barrel. He and Sergeant stand looking at one another.

SERGEANT What are you waiting for?

MAN For my hat, of course, and my wig. You wouldn't wish me to get my death of cold?

Sergeant gives them.

MAN (*going towards steps*) Well, goodnight, comrade, and thank you. You did me a good turn tonight, and I'm obliged to you. Maybe I'll be able to do as much for you when the small rise up and the big fall down..., when we all change places at the rising (*waves his hand and disappears*) of the moon.

SERGEANT (*turning his back to audience and reading placard*) A hundred pounds reward! A hundred pounds! (*turns towards audience*) I wonder, now, am I as great a fool as I think I am?

THE END

GRANUAILE

Lady Gregory

THE RISING OF THE MOON

O, then, tell me, Shawn O' Far - ell where the gath' ring is to be. In the old spot by the

ri - ver, Right well known to you and me. One word

more, for sig - nal to - ken whis - tle up the march - ing

tune, With your pike up - on your should - er at the

ris - ing of the moon.

Lady Gregory

EVERY AFTERNOON
by Gertrude Stein

*There is no list of characters or specific setting for EVERY AFTERNOON.

a dialogue

I get up.

So do you get up.

We are pleased with each other.

Why are you.

Because we are hopeful.

Have you any reason to be.

We have reason to be.

What is it.

I am not prepared to say.

Is there any change.

Naturally.

I know what you mean.

I consider that it is not necessary for me to teach languages.

It would be foolish of you to.

It would here.

It would anywhere.

I do not care about Peru.

I hope you do.

Do I begin this.

Yes you began this.

Of course we did.

Yes indeed we did.

When will we speak of another.

Not today I assure you.

Yes certainly you mentioned it.

We mentioned everything.

To another.

I do not wish reasons.

You mean you are taught early.

That is exactly what I mean.

And I feel the same.

You feel it to be the same.

Don't tempt him.

Do not tempt him.

This evening there was no question of temptation he was not the least interested.

Neither was she.

Of course she wasn't.

It's really not necessary to ask her.

I found it necessary.

You did

Certainly.

And when have you leisure.

Reading and knitting.

Reading or knitting.

Reading or knitting.

Yes reading or knitting.

In the evening.

Actively first.

He was very settled.

Where was he settled.

In Marseilles.

I cannot understand words.

Cannot you.

You are so easily deceived you don't ask what do they decide what are they to decide.

There is no reason.

No there is no reason.

Between meals.

Do you really sew.

He was so necessary to me.

We are equally pleased.

Come and stay.

Do so.

Do you mean to be rude.

Did he.

I ask you why.

Tomorrow.

Yes tomorrow.

Every afternoon.

A dialogue.

What did you do with your dog.

We sent him into the country.

Was he a trouble.

Not at all but we thought he would be better off there.

Yes it isn't right to keep a large dog in the city.

Yes I agree with you.

Yes

Coming.

Yes certainly.

Do be quick.

Not in breathing.

No you know you don't mind.

We said yes.

Come ahead.

That sounded like an animal.

Were you expecting something.

I don't know.

Don't you know about it at all.

You know I don't believe it.

She did.

Well they are different

I am not very careful.

Mention that again.

Here.

Not here.

Don't receive wood.

Don't receive wood.

Well we went and found it.

Tomorrow.

Come tomorrow.

Come tomorrow.

Yes we said yes. Come tomorrow.

Coming very well. Don't be irritable. Don't say you haven't been told. You know I want a telegram. Why. Because emperors didn't.

I don't remember that.

I don't care for a long time.

For a long time to pass away.

Why not.

Because I like him.

That's what she said.

We said.

We will gladly come Saturday.

She will go.

Oh yes she will.

What is a conversation.

We can all sing.

A great many people come in.

A great many people come in.

Why do the days pass so quickly.

Because we are very happy.

Yes that's so.

That's it.

That is it.

Who cares for daisies.

Do you hear me.

Yes I can hear you.

Very well then explain.

That I care for daisies.

That we care for daisies.

Come in come in.

Yes and I will not cry.

No indeed.

We will picnic.

Oh yes.

We are very happy.

Very happy.

And content.

And content.

We will go and hear Tito Ruffo.

Here.

Yes here.

Oh yes I remember about that. He is to be here.

To begin with what did we buy.

Scolding.

If you remember you will remember other things that frighten you.

Will I.

Yes and there is no necessity the explanation is not in your walking first of walking last of walking beside me the only reason that there is plenty of room is that

I choose it.

Then we will say that it will rain.

The other day there was bright moonlight.

Not here.

No not here but on the whole there is more moonlight than in Brittany.

Come again.

Come in again.

Coming again.

Coming in again.

Come again.

I say I do understand calling.

Calling him.

Yes Polybe.

Come.

Come.

Come again and bring a book.

We meet him so often.

We meant to see about it. You mean the light.

I am proud of her. You have every reason to be and she takes it so naturally.

It is better that it is her hands.

Yes of course.

Nothing can pay for that.

Republics are so ungrateful.

Do you desire to appear here.

Why of course in that sense.

I do not know those words.

It is really wretched.

You do see it.

I don't see it that way.

No you wouldn't you would prefer the words well and tall.

Say it to me.

You know I never wished to be blamed.

An effort to eat quickly.

Did you promise him.

Did I promise him the woods.

The woods.

Not now.

You mean not now.

THE END

About the Playwrights

Hrotsvitha (c.935 – c.1002) was a nun, poet and dramatist. Her plays are the first known works of dramatic writing since antiquity; they include: *Gallicanus*, *Callimachus*, and *Paphnutius*.

Lady Gregory (1852-1932) was an Irish dramatist, folklorist and theater manager. She co-founded the Irish Literary Theater and Abbey Theater and wrote many short works for each. Her plays include: *Cathleen Ni Houlihan*, *Spreading The News*, and *Hyacinth Halvey*.

Gertrude Stein (1874-1946) is best known for her work as an art collector and novelist. Her Paris salon was the haunt of noted figures including Hemingway, Picasso, and F. Scott Fitzgerald. Many of her plays were published in the 1922 collection *Geography and Plays*.

also available from New Muses

Lysistrata by Aristophanes

The Seagull by Anton Chekhov

A Servant of Two Masters by Carlo Goldoni

A Doll's House by Henrik Ibsen

Ghosts by Henrik Ibsen

Peer Gynt by Henrik Ibsen

Doctor Faustus by Christopher Marlowe

Tartuffe by Molière

6 Characters in Search of an Author by Luigi Pirandello

Hamlet, Prince of Denmark by William Shakespeare

Romeo & Juliet by William Shakespeare

Miss Julie by August Strindberg

Riders to the Sea & In the Shadow of the Glen by J.M. Synge

The Importance of Being Earnest by Oscar Wilde

Dulcitius, The Rising of the Moon & Every Afternoon
a trinity of plays by Hrotsvitha, Lady Gregory, and Gertrude Stein

www.NewMuses.com

Made in the USA
Columbia, SC
18 September 2024